GW00362793

NEVER GIVE UP
THE SUN WILL SHINE AGAIN

By BREEA ROSS
2007

PUBLISHED BY
ADAPT
EATING DISTRESS ASSOCIATION
2007

never give up

Never Give Up - The Sun Will Shine Again

Published by ADAPT Eating Distress Association, 2007

Copyright © ADAPT 2007

No reproduction without permission

**ADAPT is a registered Charity
No: XR43015**

ISBN 978-0-9555273-0-2

<u>Acknowledgements</u>

Author of this book - Breea Ross, SRN. DIP. Eating Disorders Practitioner.

Adapt would like to thank Investing for Mental Health at Mental Health & Social Services Trust for the Grant that made it possible to write and publish this book.

Adapt would also like to thank Colin Loughran, who helped in the layout and design of the book. Patricia and Diana, Administrators, for their patience and support. Also, the ADAPT Committee for their time and expertise with this project.

CONTENTS

Adapt

Mission Statement

To increase knowledge and a greater understanding of eating distress in the community.

To provide help and support to people with eating disorders, their families and friends.

To lobby local and regional organisations and advocate on behalf of sufferers and carers of eating distress.

BACKGROUND

ADAPT is a voluntary registered charitable organisation which promotes greater understanding and awareness of Eating Distress, such as Anorexia and Bulimia Nervosa. Established in January 2000, Adapt has grown to become one of the primary support organisations for eating disorders in Northern Ireland.

Services include:

- **Telephone** help line/general information line;

- **Website**: information on various aspects of "Eating Distress" including healthy eating, body image and self-esteem;

- **Education** and awareness-raising work with schools, community groups, youth clubs and the public;

- **Training**: Specialist Eating Distress Training for volunteers, carers, sufferers, health professionals and teachers;

- **Drop-in centre** where people can call for a chat, by appointment; Outreach work 1+1 on request by our professional "Eating Disorders practitioner";

- **Self-help monthly support groups** (separate groups for sufferers and carers);

- **Information** packs and leaflets.

EATING DISTRESS: THE FACTS

Facts about Eating Disorders

- Eating disorder rates are on the increase - and have doubled in the last decade.

- Eating disorders are not about food but about feelings and a crisis of identity and self-worth.

- An estimated 1,700 people in Northern Ireland suffer from Anexoria, while 17,000 are currently battling with Bulimia.

- Eating disorders are increasingly being found in primary school children.

- 30% of children with anexoria are boys.

- 10% of adult sufferers are male.

- One in ten anorexics die from the condition or from suicide.

- Most people with bulimia keep their condition completely secret.

INTERESTING FACTS ABOUT BODIES, DIETING AND EATING DISORDERS:

- Eating disorders affect about half a million people at any given time.

- 8-12% of the population have bulimia.

- 6-10% of those with an eating disorder die, usually from a heart attack.

- 80% of the female population have dieted before reaching the age of 18.

- About 20% of women aged 18-29 are trying to lose weight even though they are not overweight.

- Women need a fat level of approximately 22% of body weight to menstruate normally.

- Most diets fail (over 90%) in the long run because healthy eating patterns have not been established.

- Health risks are mainly associated with extreme obesity but not with being a few pounds overweight.

- 1 in 10,000 females naturally (without dieting) meet model-thin dimensions.

- Thin does not equal fit. You can be heavy and fit.

- Excessive dieting can lead to irratability, depression and withdrawal.

PREVENTION OF EATING DISORDERS: ADVICE FOR PARENTS

Preventing eating disorders is one way that eating disorders can be fought before they begin. Being *aware* of eating disorders and making others aware of these terrible diseases and the impact they have on one's life is one way we can stop others from following in the footsteps of so many. A few simple measures could make all the difference between life and death.

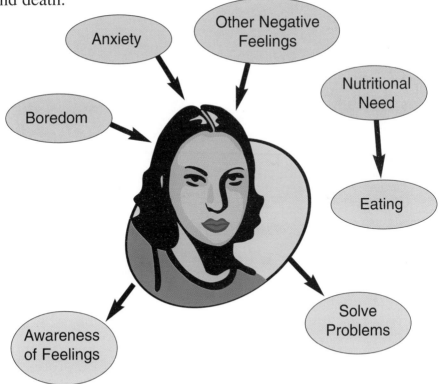

Education is the best tool we have against eating disorders.

Self-esteem

Building a positive, healthy self-esteem is something that starts from the day we are born and helps us through our life. Help your children build a positive self-esteem about the way they are. This is something you can do on a daily basis. Teach your sons and daughters about self-respect, and teach them to value who they are, or even what they do. The better they feel about themselves, the happier they will turn out to be. Once a healthy self-esteem is established, the more confident they will be to do well and the less chance there will be of their developing eating distress.

Diets

Talk to your children about the harms and benefits of dieting. Let them know why people want to lose weight and how it can be done in healthy ways. If your child has had a problem of being overweight and expresses the desire to diet, take her/him to your health care provider, who will help to set up a safe and healthy diet programme for your child.

Exercising

Let your children know the benefits of exercising and fitness, and that too little exercise is as bad as too much. Teach them to exercise for the good feelings it brings to stay fit and flexible and *not* to burn fat from the body nor burn off food they have eaten. Make sure they exercise for the right reason and in moderation.

Prejudice

As a parent, try to convey the fact that different people have different shapes. Don't tease or make jokes about an overweight person, as this will indirectly teach your children that fat means ugly. Try to avoid saying things like: "she'd look better if she lost weight" or "she's too fat". Teach your children that there is more to a person than body shape and beauty, that beauty comes from within and that we shouldn't judge people just from how they look on the outside.

Nutrition

Teach your children healthy eating habits at home. You can talk about what kinds of foods are good for them and the importance of eating three well-balanced meals a day. Through education you can let your children know the importance of food to the body, that it is essential for growth, energy and overall health and happiness. Do not limit the calories they take in unless advised by a physician. Let them know that eating and having a good, healthy appetite is okay. Try not to label foods in your home as fattening, bad, good, dangerous, etc. Teach them to eat sensibly and healthily.

Fruit and vegetables

Bread, other cereals and potatoes

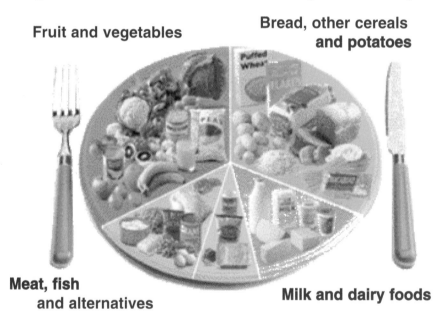

Meat, fish and alternatives

Milk and dairy foods

Foods containing fat
Foods containing sugar

Source: The Food Standards Agency

8

Very Unhealthy Body Mass

Healthy Body Mass

Advertising

These days more than ever, children are exposed to television and magazines and the ways in which they portray the human body. Talk to your children about what they see on television and in magazines. Let them know that being slim and thin does not mean power and is not the only acceptable image. Also let them know that what they see isn't always as it appears. Models can be made out to seem thinner than they really are. Make your children aware that behind the fancy clothes and make-up, models are just as normal as they are.

WHAT ARE EATING DISORDERS?

Eating disorders are not primarily about food starving or binge eating. These are symptoms of underlying emotional and psychological disorders that involve very serious abnormalities in eating.

Eating disorders include anorexia nervosa and bulimia nervosa, binge eating, compulsive overeating, and obsessional behaviour around food. Eating distress can sometimes be accompanied by excessive exercising. For some people eating disorders become the way in which they try to cope with life when they experience, seemingly insoluble, problems.

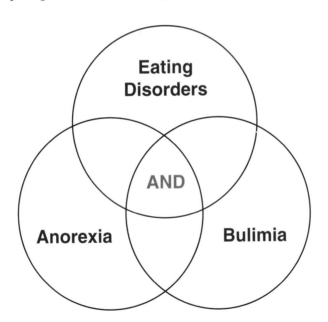

Anorexia nervosa was first named as a clinical entity in the 19th century and bulimia nervosa in the 1970s.

Eating Disorders: a vicious circle of self-abuse

Self-starvation can lead to obsessive thinking and compulsive behaviours centred on food and eating

As less is eaten, the stomach shrinks and the person feels full more quickly when eating.

As the person becomes more fixated on refusing food, in attempts to "correct" his/her body image, the disorder worsens.

Anexoria Nervosa Cycle of Self-abuse

The person's already distorted body image worsens.

The resulting loss of muscle causes the stomach to protrude

Fluid retention and bloating follow, further reinforcing these fears.

The person's perception, fantasies and fears of fatness are now reinforced.

Both anorexia nervosa and bulimia nervosa can have serious effects on all aspects of a person's life - physical, emotional, social - and in extreme cases can cause death. It is estimated that, in Ireland, there are 10,000 people between the ages of 14 and 20 who have eating disorders. There are many more people in their 20s, 30s, 40s and older who suffer from eating disorders and also many people under the age of 14 who develop anorexia, although the likeliest time is in the teens and early twenties.

Anorexia affects your whole body

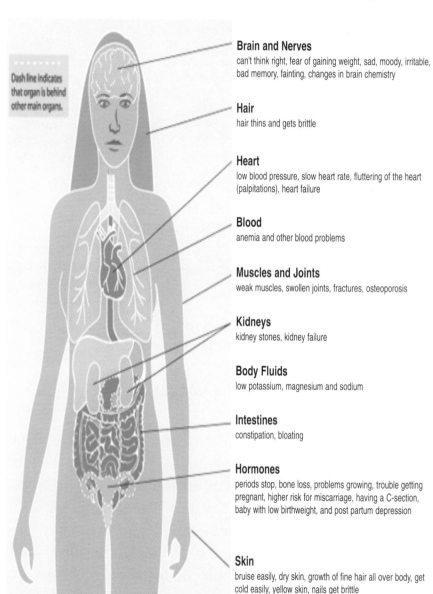

Dash line indicates that organ is behind other main organs.

Brain and Nerves
can't think right, fear of gaining weight, sad, moody, irritable, bad memory, fainting, changes in brain chemistry

Hair
hair thins and gets brittle

Heart
low blood pressure, slow heart rate, fluttering of the heart (palpitations), heart failure

Blood
anemia and other blood problems

Muscles and Joints
weak muscles, swollen joints, fractures, osteoporosis

Kidneys
kidney stones, kidney failure

Body Fluids
low potassium, magnesium and sodium

Intestines
constipation, bloating

Hormones
periods stop, bone loss, problems growing, trouble getting pregnant, higher risk for miscarriage, having a C-section, baby with low birthweight, and post partum depression

Skin
bruise easily, dry skin, growth of fine hair all over body, get cold easily, yellow skin, nails get brittle

ANOREXIA NERVOSA

Dieting is a common feature of Western life. All of us at some stage will want to lose some weight and many of us will go on a diet. Dieting of this nature is extremely common amongst teenage girls and should not cause any concern. Anorexia nervosa, however, results from an interaction of several factors and is not a result of dieting. This disorder (distress) is a form of self imposed starvation most common among the female population in their early to mid teens.

What is Anorexia Nervosa?

"Anorexia nervosa" is a medical term which in translation means a "nervous loss of appetite". The literal translation of the term is in actual fact misleading since the sufferer does not lose an interest in food. She will in fact have a normal appetite and may indeed display a preoccupation with food/eating and, in many cases, intensive exercise. Indeed, as the sufferer's body weight falls, her preoccupation with food will increase. Anorexia nervosa is perhaps more accurately defined as an emotional disorder (distress), which is characterized by a distorted perception of weight and shape which leads to an obsessive control of food intake and body weight.

How is Anorexia Nervosa identified?

The physical signs of anorexia nervosa include:

- A severely reduced body weight
- Cessation of menstruation or amenorrhoea in women.

Although it is generally overall physical symptoms which will bring the anorexic patient to the attention of the medical profession, these symptoms can be associated with a number of other diseases. The family doctor will conduct a physical examination.

In order to identify anorexia, the physical symptoms must be considered in conjunction with the behaviour and the psychological attitude.

The sufferer will tend to avoid food that she considers to be fattening. She may, as a result, eat quantities of low calorie foods to mask the meagre calorie intake. Other weight control methods may also be employed, self-induced vomiting or excessive exercise for example. In general the sufferer will strive to maintain her abnormally thin, often gaunt appearance. It is not unusual for the signs of anorexia nervosa to remain unobserved by family and friends for quite some time.

You can overcome it

What are the physical effects of this disorder/distress?

The characteristic low calorie intake associated with this disorder/distress will ultimately take its toll upon the body. Those suffering from anorexia may experience problems sleeping, their blood pressure may reach a dangerously low level and in some cases the reduction in body temperature, which is related to the low calorie intake, may lead to the development of fine downy hair (Lanugo) on the face and neck. As body weight falls bodily functions will generally slow down.

What treatment is available?

In the case of anorexia it is generally a relative or friend who will identify the problem. It is essential that it is identified and treated as quickly as possible if hospitalisation is to be avoided. The sufferer should be examined by a general practitioner, who will conduct a physical examination to establish the possibility of the presence of the illness.

If anexoria is suspected, the general practitioner will then be able to refer the sufferer to a psychiatrist or psychologist. The professionals in conjunction with the sufferer would agree on a targeted diet as well as helping her to understand why the problem started.

In many cases the sufferer may not accept that she has a problem, she may not even acknowledge that she is too thin. Skilled help is essential if recovery is to be made possible.

It's not your Fault
You're not Alone
We can Help

MALE SUFFERERS

The misconception that anorexia nervosa is a disorder affecting exclusively young women must be almost as widespread as the mistaken view that it is a "slimming disease". It is estimated that approximately 5-10% of a anorexia nervosa sufferers are male.

Despite greater media interest in recent years and public awareness of anorexia and bulimia as serious health problems, a considerable number of male sufferers remain unknown to the medical profession, self-help groups and other support structures. This is partly due to reluctance on the sufferer's part to seek help, together with a strong denial that anything may be wrong. In addition, many health professionals do not consider anorexia nervosa a possible diagnosis in males and are surprised or disbelieving about the existence of male sufferers. Boys as young as 11 or 12 may become anorexic, though the disorder is one to which women are very much more vulnerable.

Adapt is here to help you, you are not alone.

Marilyn Lawrence of the Women's Therapy Centre puts it well when she says: "anorexia is a problem crucially related to women's psychology, which in turn is related to women's way of being in  the world. The fact that it sometimes affects men only indicates that the psychology of women and men is not wholly distinct: issues problematic for most women can also be so for some men".

Recent research has shown that male and female sufferers have similar personalities and symptoms, except that men seem more achievement-oriented and show more sexual anxiety. In general, they also appear to be excessively athletic and overvalue physical fitness, body appearance and muscle strength. Not every male fits this picture, although all do show the weight loss and eating difficulties characteristic of anorexia nervosa.

The first step towards recovery is to recognise the problem and to realise that one must begin where one is. There has to be a genuine desire to get better, which may involve profound changes in lifestyle and circumstances. There needs to be an exploration, understanding and resolution of the underlying issues and feelings alongside a re-shaping of attitudes to food and weight. Realistic targets must be set so that periods spent "treading water" or in relapse are kept short.

Recovery is possible, although it is often hard work and the process of re-building can be emotionally charged as well as lengthy. But once the energy trapped in anorexia/bulimia begins to be released into all other areas of the sufferer's life, his family and community wonderful things happen.

Books

"Anorexia Nervosa: A Guide For Sufferers And Their Families" by R. Palmer, published by Penguin, is suitable for readers of both sexes;

D. Scott's *"Anorexia and Bulimia Nervosa: Practical Approaches"* (Croom Helm, 1988) has a chapter about males;

Dally, Gomex & Isaacs *"Anorexia Nervosa"* (1979) pp. 142-151.

BULIMIA NERVOSA

Bulimia Nervosa is a medical term which in translation means an 'insatiable hunger'. This eating disorder (distress), most common among women in their early to mid twenties, is associated with overpowering urges to eat large amounts of food in a relatively short period of time followed by self-induced vomiting or purging with laxatives.

The condition 'bulimia nervosa' is dominated by binge eating and like 'anorexia nervosa' originates from an abnormal fear of becoming fat. Bulimia nervosa may develop as a phase of anorexia, particularly during the recovery process. The anexoria sufferer may turn to vomiting or purging with laxatives when they feel they have eaten too much or simply exceeded what they consider to be their normal food intake. Through time the sufferer may come to regard vomiting/purging with laxatives as a means of counteracting the effects of overeating and weight gain.

This process can all too easily become habit-forming and indeed, may help to alleviate pressure from family and friends as the sufferer appears to be eating normally, and confrontations are thus avoided. It is, as a result, not uncommon for this situation to continue undetected for months, even years.

What are the physical symptoms of Bulimia?

In contrast to anorexia, the person suffering from bulimia is successful in maintaining a body weight within what is considered to be normal boundaries (based upon individual height). This disorder (distress) is, as a result, difficult to identify.

The physical effects of Bulimia Nervosa, however, may include:

- Dermatitis around the mouth
- Swollen salivary glands
- Chronic sore throat
- Dental problems due to deterioration of tooth enamel by stomach acid (extreme cases)
- Constipation and dehydration caused by a lack of carbohydrates and potassium in the diet, a direct result of continued vomiting/purging
- Irregular heartbeat
- Kidney damage
- Persistent stomach pain
- Bowel damage

Diagnosis of this disorder (distress) is not based solely upon the physical symptoms but in conjunction with the psychological and behavioural attitudes of the suspected sufferer. Many bulimia sufferers also display symptoms of depression.

Do Bulimia sufferers need to be hospitalised?

In the absence of serious medical complications or psychological problems, hospitalisation is generally unnecessary. Part of the treatment for this disorder (distress) is relearning how to establish a normal eating pattern in the sufferer's own environment. Hospitalisation may, as a result, hinder the recovery process.

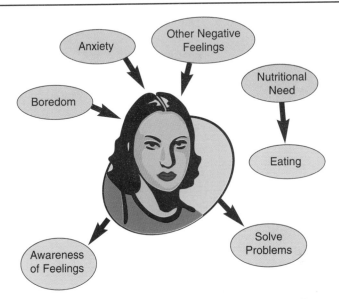

What treatment is available for Bulimia Nervosa?

The first step towards recovery from bulimia, as is the case in all eating disorders (distress), is recognition of the fact that a problem actually exists. In many cases it can be a great relief for the Bulimia sufferer to finally admit to the disorder (distress). Having identified the problem, the sufferer should first consult a general practitioner, who will be able to make a referral to a psychiatrist or psychologist.

You can get better. Recovery is possible even after many years of illness.

other eating disorders

COMPULSIVE EATING

Many people who classify themselves as "compulsive eaters" may be medically diagnosed as "binge-eaters". This group of people can be helped more by counselling, cognitive behaviour therapies and other talking treatments than by dieting.

Other symptoms often include:

- weight obsession
- occasional food binges
- yo-yo dieting leading to the possession of two wardrobes of significantly different sizes
- periods of strict dieting
- use of food to numb negative feelings followed by guilt
- predominant nibbling

Over Eaters share similar psychological problems with people who have anorexia and bulimia and may find the help offered by Adapt Eating Distress Association useful.

Adapt does not offer diets and does not help people with weight reduction. Children and adolescents with eating disorders should be treated by child and adolescent specialists who also have expertise in treating eating disorders.

FAMILIES AND FRIENDS

Family and friends often recognise that "something is wrong" long before the person concerned is prepared to acknowledge that they have a problem. Parents can therefore feel "at their wits end", having all their concerns and suggestions denied and rejected. The home can often become a battleground where food becomes a powerful weapon. Eating disorders have a ripple effect throughout families, causing much distress and putting relationships under pressure.

Families and friends can greatly benefit from having support for themselves during this time. Adapt is there to give help/support and understanding. By knowing more about eating disorders, families can learn how to clarify their own boundaries and, in so doing, learn how to more effectively help and support the person who is ill.

never, never, ever give up

never, never, ever give up

CAUSES AND TRIGGERS OF EATING DISTRESS

- Low self-esteem
- Bullying
- Difficulty with family relationships
- Academic pressures
- Moving away from home
- Bereavement
- Pressure to lose weight
- Difficulty in dealing with the changes of adolescence
- Sexual or emotional abuse
- Feeling of not being in control of one's life

It is important not to try to reduce weight too quickly as that stirs up ***feelings of hunger and the temptation to start bingeing again.***

There are many reasons why people binge but ***low self-esteem is one of the main ones.***

Low self-esteem

Self-esteem is the opinion an individual has about him/herself. People with eating difficulties often dislike themselves leading to low self-esteem.

Self-esteem also involves self-confidence in our abilities and we can be influenced by what others think about us.

Bullying

A person is bullied when he or she is exposed regularly, and over time, to negative actions on the part of one or more persons. It involves an imbalance of power - the powerful attacking the powerless. It can be verbal, physical or psychological in nature.

Difficulty with family relationships

People with eating distress often have great difficulty in managing relationships of all kinds. They are generally insecure and depend on the approval of others as they have little sense of self-worth or value. Some children and teenagers find saying no to food is the only way they can make their feelings felt and have influence in the family. Formal counselling or therapy can help the individual identify and resolve emotional issues associated with the eating problem so that personal change becomes possible. This may involve talking through painful experiences from the past or discussing relationship problems past or present.

Academic pressures

Sometimes when students are under pressure, e.g. coming up to exams or assignment dates, the first thing they forget to do is eat. They often neglect their physical well being by not eating the right food and not getting enough sleep. This leads to poor concentration, poor retention of revision work and then, ultimately, a sense of panic that in itself can often reduce the appetite.

Moving away from home

Where many young people enjoy the freedom from parental influence, very often problems can appear after a short time. Where eating problems did exist and parents or close family friends supported the person at home, now they find they are on their own and have to take this responsibility on. Some find this responsibility too much to cope with and their physical and mental health deteriorate. This is why it is important to have someone to contact for help and support.

Bereavement

When you lose someone close to you, it will affect you mentally and physically. Your everyday routine is initially disrupted. You may feel a variety of unpleasant emotions and try to cope by talking a lot, being restless, moving about aimlessly and trying to find something to do. However, you may also revert into yourself and often the appetite is suppressed because of your stress and pain.

Pressure to lose weight

We are surrounded by what the media sees as "the perfect body". Sadly, the reality is often a picture of a painfully thin and unhealthy person. Also pressure from family or GP to lose weight, maybe for health reasons, can lead to an erratic eating pattern. We all want to fit in, but unfortunately for some, control over food and weight becomes their life.

Difficulty in dealing with the changes of adolescence

Adolescents can feel insecure about themselves and worried about growing up. This can involve their bodies developing, school changes and developing relationships. Some adolescents find this so difficult that they stop eating to try and slow down this process. As well as maybe developing an eating disorder, they can often develop other medical problems.

Sexual or emotional abuse

Anorexia and bulimia thrive in our culture. Some young people are terrified of being large, and sexual abuse then compounds this problem. Many girls who have been sexually abused begin to suffer from anorexia when they go through puberty. **Anorexia, like compulsive eating, is an attempt to protect you, to assert control. By strictly controlling what you do and don't take into your body, you are trying to regain the power that was taken from you as a child.**

A feeling of not being in control of one's life
Socially, people with eating distress become more and more isolated as their mental state revolves increasingly around food and weight control. As a result, they are sometimes unable to cope with social situations.

BODY IMAGE AND SELF-ESTEEM
When we are young, body image gets especially complicated, especially during adolescence when our bodies really begin to change. Adolescents are often over-sensitive towards their bodies during the onset of puberty. Over-exposure to the media directs young people to examine their bodies and even measure their physical appearance against unrealistic, computer-enhanced images.

Adolescent years are often full of confusion, self-doubt and the search for an identity, compounded by dramatic physical changes taking place in the body.

Most of us focus on things we don't like about our bodies. We tend to overlook totally the fact that we have good bits as well. If we say negative things often enough to ourselves we really start to believe them and in turn find it even harder to say something in praise of ourselves.

What causes an image problem?

Poor body image can be brought about in lots of different ways and under the influence of key people in our lives, e.g. parents, friends, boyfriends/girlfriends. It can also be caused by those whose main interest is self-interest, e.g. the media and the diet industry.

What can you do about your self-image *today*? The first step is to realise that there are things that you can change and things you can't. Make a list of the things you can change and the things you can't change. Develop an action plan to help you work on the things you can change. Set yourself realistic goals and work at your own pace to achieve these goals. If you make a decision to change something you dislike, remember the following:

- It won't make all your other problems disappear.
- It won't happen overnight.
- If your plan does not work first time, try again.
- Working towards your goal at your own pace is more likely to end in success.

The things that can't be changed are a fundamental part of you. You can choose to accept them or to let them get you down. Accepting them won't mean that you'll become instantly and blissfully happy but it will mean that you can stop blaming the "unchangeables" for all your misfortunes.

Reinforcing the good

On a big sheet of paper write down all your good points and don't let false modesty hold you back. Pin this list above the mirror in your room, read it regularly and update it. Take a good look at your list and imagine that someone else had all these traits. Would you like them? Would you want to be friends with them? Of course you would. Accepting who you are "warts and all" will increase your self-esteem and give you:

- a firm belief in your own abilities
- a feeling that you've got something to offer the world
- a positive attitude that you can be and do whatever you work at
- the strength to resist those who may try to control your life
- an inner belief in yourself so that the comments and opinions of others won't get you down
- the courage to overcome fear of failure.

Finally, remember:

If you like yourself, you will like others.
If you respect yourself, you will respect others.
If you accept that nothing is perfect, you won't ask for perfection in others.
To make the world a better place, you have to start with yourself and work outwards.

Seeing your body in a positive way will improve your outlook and how you respond to other people. Remember, until you learn to respect your body as much as your mind, behaviour and attitudes, you will never wholly respect yourself.

The benefits of a positive body image

- You'll glow with inner confidence, feel good about yourself and accept that even a most precious diamond has flaws.

- You'll know that you are unique and will therefore stop comparing yourself to anyone else (especially super models).

- You'll say goodbye to "bad hair days". No longer will spots or unruly hair rule your mood, turning potential good times into nightmares.

- You'll no longer be so critical of your friends. By accepting that everyone is unique and by being proud of yourself, you will stop being "Little Miss/Mister Critical".

- You'll become more comfortable around others and no longer hide behind chairs worrying that someone will notice you. Instead, you'll be mingling and making chitchat.

- "Get thin" fads and crash diets will pass you by. Your body is a temple and you'll do nothing to harm it.

- Words will never hurt you again. Those nasty, uncaring comments that once would have made you cry for a week will no longer bother you. Because you are more level-headed you'll accept fair criticism when you recognise it's for your own good.

WHAT SELF-ESTEEM IS . . . and IS NOT

SELF-Esteem is:

- ✓ Feeling worthy
- ✓ Being in control of your own destiny
- ✓ Taking responsibility for your behaviour
- ✓ Loving yourself unconditionally
- ✓ Believing in yourself
- ✓ Being willing to take calculated risks
- ✓ Setting goals and working to achieve them
- ✓ Recognising your accomplishments and celebrate successes
- ✓ Asking for what you want

SELF-Esteem is not:

✓ Showing arrogance

✓ Being afraid of change

✓ Being preoccupied with "doing" rather than "being"

✓ Blaming others for your actions

✓ Expecting things in your life to be perfect

✓ Taking advantage of other people

✓ Being preoccupied by what you "should" be doing

✓ Being afraid of success

SELF-ESTEEM

Building a positive, healthy self-esteem is something that starts from the day we are born and helps us through our life. Help your children build a positive self-esteem about the way they are. This is something you can do on a daily basis. Teach your sons and daughters about self-respect, and teach them to value who they are, or even what they do. The better they feel about themselves, the happier they will turn out to be. Once a healthy self-esteem is established, the more confident they will be to do well and the less chance there will be of their developing eating distress.

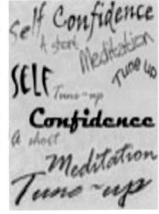

STEPS to SELF-ESTEEM

Self-esteem is something that can be learned and developed over time. Following are some of the ways in which you can enhance your self-esteem:

✓ Become knowledgeable about the topic of self-esteem
✓ Hang out with people who have high self-esteem
✓ Face your fears about change
✓ Connect with your strengths
✓ Recognise personal pitfalls that lower your self-esteem
  - Specific people?
  - Words?
  - Certain decisions?
  - Behaviours?
✓ Set realistic daily goals
✓ Recognise all your accomplishments and celebrate your successes
✓ Identify your true mission in life
✓ Learn to love yourself
✓ Deal with pain from your past
✓ Make informed decisions
✓ Answer the question "Why am I here?"
✓ Believe in yourself

WORRIED ABOUT A YOUNG PERSON'S EATING?

YOUNG PEOPLE AND EATING PROBLEMS

People's eating habits vary but serious problems with eating can have a damaging effect on physical and emotional health. People vary a great deal in the way that they eat. Some eat a lot or eat anything; others are more particular. Some people can only get going after a good breakfast and others cannot face a meal until later in the day.

These differences are to be expected and usually should not be a cause for concern. For example, younger children often refuse to eat certain foods and teenagers may go through food fads. Most of us have carried out a diet at some time in our lives, whether to slim a little or put on some weight, or to improve our health.

But some eating problems are serious and can have a damaging effect on physical and emotional health. The most common of these "eating disorders" are anorexia nervosa, bulimia nervosa and compulsive eating. Eating disorders affect many more girls than boys but it is important to remember that boys *do* suffer from them too.

Anorexia nervosa

People with anorexia nervosa have an extreme fear of normal body weight and feel fat, even when they have lost so much weight that it becomes obvious to others. They may starve themselves by only eating tiny quantities of food, especially salads, fruit and vegetables. Some stubbornly and angrily resist attempts to get them to eat a proper diet, or pretend to have eaten when they have not. A girl's periods may stop. Many sufferers exercise vigorously in order to lose more weight. Nevertheless, a fascination with food and cooking for others is common.

Bulimia nervosa

Bulimia tends to affect slightly older people, although adolescents do suffer from it. People with bulimia gorge themselves with food in "binges" and then make themselves sick to get rid of the food. They might also take large amounts of laxatives. They may not look overweight or underweight, which can make their eating problems difficult to detect. Continuous bingeing and vomiting can eventually do serious harm to the body.

Compulsive eating

People who eat compulsively consume much more food than their bodies need over a long period, or use food to comfort or distract themselves. They may become very overweight, which can lead to serious medical problems.

Starting young

Problems with food often show during adolescence and often signify that a young person is feeling troubled. These problems should be taken seriously. As well as having an adverse effect on a young person's physical health, eating disorders are often a sign that something is troubling them emotionally.

Eating disorders may be linked, for example, to unhappiness at home, pressures at school or major changes to family life. Feelings of loss through bereavement or divorce could be a trigger, as could the shock and distress suffered by a child who has been abused. Sometimes social pressure to be thin and conform to an unrealistic ideal results in excessive dieting. Growing up can be a frightening experience for some; anorexia can slow down physical development and thus seem to delay becoming an adult. Some young people with eating problems may see their weight as the only part of their lives over which they have control.

Without help, eating disorders can damage young people's bodies and can leave them feeling bad about themselves, guilty and depressed. There is a small but definite risk of suicide. Eating disorders can also affect future health. For example, anorexia in the teenage years can cause infertility and osteoporosis (brittle bones) in adult life. However, sufferers may deny that they have a problem or try to keep it a secret, and may find it difficult to accept that they need help.

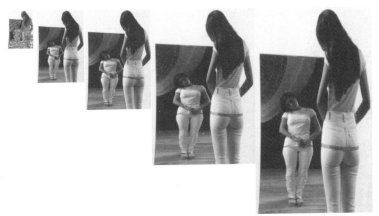

Recognising eating problems

There are a number of signs, which may be a cause for concern. It can sometimes be hard for parents and other adults who have regular contact with young people to spot eating disorders. Below are some pointers, which do not necessarily indicate an eating disorder but may suggest a problem.

- Regularly skipping meals
- Obsessively counting calories

- Eating only low-calorie food
- Avoid interest in buying or cooking food for others
- Wearing very loose clothes to hide the body
- An obsession with exercise
- Dramatic weight loss or gain
- Food missing in large amounts from the fridge/larder
- Disappearing from the table directly after meals (in order to make themselves vomit)

What can be done to help?

Eating disorders tend to get worse if they are not treated, so it is important to get help early on. A GP will be able to refer the young person to a mental health professional specialising in this area. Treatment will be based around a combination of dietary control and the resolution of any underlying problems, and may involve therapy for the whole family. If the sufferer has lost a great deal of weight or other help seems not to work, they may spend some time in hospital or a special unit where treatment can be more closely monitored. Young people unwilling to accept help through their parents may be able to refer themselves to a counsellor. Many areas have specialist youth counselling services.

Treat comments about food/weight with humour rather than taking it to heart. Look at where the other person is coming from, i.e. are they concerned/jealous/trying to hurt you?

never give up

If you must have alcohol, ensure that you have something to eat first, as alcohol lowers blood sugar levels and creates a craving for food.

Instead of bingeing/purging/starving to deal with problems, think of alternative ways of coping, i.e.

• Boredom - plan pleasurable activities

• Stress - use stress management techniques such as relaxation

• Disappointment - share your feelings

• Unassertiveness - it's OK to say "no".

Keep in mind the effects of your behaviour on physical, mental and social aspects of self, plus the effects on others.

COPING WITH FOOD INTAKE

Ensure a regular eating pattern as starving creates a need to binge.

Starving all day, then eating at night, causes wind to gather and this causes a bloated feeling at night, even when little is consumed.

Starving all day only leads to the feeling of inability to stop eating when you eventually do eat. The body tries to make up for what it didn't get during the day.

Remember you don't have to eat everything. By wearing loose clothing you will feel more comfortable following meals.

The Balance of Good Health

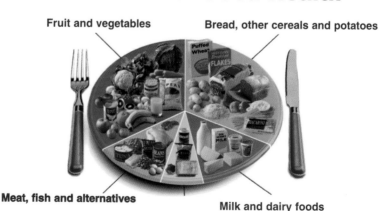

Fruit and vegetables

Bread, other cereals and potatoes

Meat, fish and alternatives

Milk and dairy foods

Foods containing fat
Foods and drinks containing sugar

There are five main groups of valuable foods

Source: Food Standards Agency

Listen to your body and be aware of how hungry you are and when you are satisfied.

Get rid of the forbidden food list. There are no good or bad foods.

Enlist the help of others. In advance tell them what would be helpful and use strategies to distract yourself after a meal.

Use relaxation techniques to help reduce the panic about eating

Minimum buying - only buy what is necessary and don't stockpile.

Don't avoid treats. Depriving yourself only sets up thoughts of food and craving.

THINK

DROP THE FAD DIETS

The secret to looking and feeling great is to make permanent lifestyle changes.

Another "wonder" diet promoted yet again by a national newspaper.

What is the attraction of those regimes with their unrealistic PROMISES "guaranteeing" readers a new body in 4-6 weeks?

Diet plans sell because they hold out the tantalising prospect of a relatively easy, quick-fix solution for people dissatisfied with their weight.

THE CATCH IS, THOUGH, THAT THERE IS NO SUCH THING AS A QUICK FIX.

Sure, if you change and improve you might lose weight for a time.

- BUT THE HARSH TRUTH IS THAT OVER THE LONG TERM, DIETS SIMPLY DON'T WORK.

- DIETING STARVES THE BODY, WHICH REACTS BY SLOWING DOWN ITS METABOLISM.

Eventually, instead of burning stored fat, the body gets used to working on fewer calories. If a dieter then increases his or her calorie intake even slightly, the extra calories join the fat stores because the body's slowed down metabolism no longer requires them.

IT IS A REALLY VICIOUS CIRCLE.

Therefore, if you really want to lose all excess weight and permanently improve your body shape, you have to think - then act - long term. It is the antithesis of 4, 6 or 8 week diet plans.

But many people don't like the thought of permanent change. They prefer to think they only have to discipline themselves for a few weeks or months before resuming all their bad habits. If they do this though, they end up not only weighing even more, but with a battered immune system and weakened resolve.

Endless features about this week's "wonder diet" only increase people's confusion and lethargy about healthy eating. They also regularly contradict themselves. One week a particular diet is said to "really work", the next it is ridiculed as rubbish or dangerous or a combination of both. People end up not knowing what to believe.

• What we eat affects what we feel, how we look, and how we function. It affects the shape and feel of our bodies, our sexuality and self-confidence, body odour, breath, skin and health. It has a major influence on concentration levels and energy and the very last thing we should be doing is messing around with fad diets.

• Not only are they unrealistic and often unhealthy, they are also frequently physically traumatic, especially when you can't stick to any one plan for more than a week or two. By their very nature, diets emphasise what we can't have, driving us into resentment and depression. Human nature being what it is, we inevitably give in to temptations and often end up eating double the quantity.

What you alone must do you cannot do alone.

All this occurs because most of us just don't know enough about all the delicious, healthy food we can eat.

Good nutrition shouldn't be about "giving up" or "doing without". That's entirely the wrong approach. Rather, it is about doing what works for long enough to see and enjoy the full results. But that is another world and is something most of us have to be shown how to enjoy.

HOW DIETING AFFECTS US

What is a slimming diet? It is a plan, a set of rules, a routine, and a regime that restricts calories in order to reduce weight. Ninety-five per cent of all dieters will regain their lost weight in one to five years. In most cases, they gain not only their former weight back, but they will also add extra pounds.

Many people on a diet reject their perfectly normal bodies as abnormally heavy. A person with an average body size who feels *fat* can have just as much body conflict as one who is actually overweight. Dieting is a deprivation and creates its own emotional hunger. When a person takes back their control and responsibilities and gets to know him or herself better, they will start to see and be able to accept positive changes in their body size.

In the USA over $40 billion is spent in dieting and diet-related products each year. The media feed us with a diet of pessimism, hopelessness and bad news. They glorify negativity and sensationalism while discouraging hope and installing fear. For this we pay a lot of money!

This myth of beauty is artificially kept alive by propaganda that encourages the false belief that being slim and dieting improves lives. We are not informed of the negative physical and emotional effects. Dieting magnifies the importance of food, causing obsessions, fears, guilt and shame that remain long after the diet is over. Dieting also distorts hunger awareness and leads to lethargy, anxiety, irritability and depression.

Bookshops are full of diet books, yet the number of people suffering with obesity is growing rapidly. There are many social pressures which promote dietary restraint. A few examples include: books and magazines containing keys to calorie counting; the fashion industry catering for the slimmer figure; the film and TV industries sending messages that a svelte figure is associated with sexuality and professional success; advertisements and feminist politics endorsing unreal role models; and even health professionals and some medical researchers emphasising physical fitness and athleticism. **Health and well-being needs to be promoted rather than appearance.**

Studies have shown that the traditional pear shape of a women, although currently devalued, is a shape associated with health. Dr. Kalucy, a leading expert on weight loss, instructs all his obese patients to stop dieting and they subsequently lose weight.

Dieting can become an addiction.

HOW TO HELP YOURSELF

- Admit the problem to yourself and then tell someone. Asking for help as soon as possible leads to a better chance of recovery.

- Keep a diary of your eating habits and feelings. This is to monitor your eating habits prior to introducing any changes to your daily food intake.

- Do not miss meals if you are not hungry.

- Don't "graze", i.e. eating small amounts frequently, keeping you topped up. This will help you to eat meals at their proper time.

- Plan meals ahead.

- Try and break habits associated with weight-reducing diets such as drinking lots of black coffee or diet coke.

- Learn to distinguish emotional needs from physical hunger, e.g. if you feel like bingeing, ask yourself: "Am I really physically hungry?"

- Don't weigh yourself excessively.

- Try to identify triggers and danger times when you are vulnerable to cutting back on food, binge eating or purging.

- Be truthful!

THINGS TO DO INSTEAD OF BINGEING/PURGING

- Go for a walk
- Relax, practice meditation
- Practice new behaviours and activities, e.g. yoga
- Make new rules such as "No eating in the car"
- Remove binge foods from the house
- Eat without combining reading, working, watching TV
- Talk to yourself: *"What is the pay-off for bingeing this time?" "What do I need that I'm not getting?"*
- Leave your binge environment, especially when frustrated, under pressure, stressed or bored
- Begin an enjoyable task or project immediately after eating a meal
- Get enough sleep and expand positive relationships
- Carry food to work or school rather than buying it there; pack healthy, satisfying food
- Work on your perfectionism. It is OK not to be perfect about every external thing
- Getting on the scales every day does not help
- Learn to like yourself
- Be aware of trigger situations and take steps to avoid them

SELF-HELP/
SUPPORT GROUP

SUFFERERS
& CARERS

Why join a self-help group?

Through joining a self-help group each member will be offered the support of others who are going through the same experience and have the same ideals. It is always encouraging to know that you are not alone. This can be particularly vital for those lacking the encouragement and emotional support of an immediate family circle.

Self-help enables people to help others while helping themselves. Through the sharing of experiences, group members are given the opportunity to learn from others whilst gaining an insight into their own difficulties.

A self-help group will give those who join the chance to speak openly and honestly about the problems they are facing with no threat of being ridiculed or doubted. It is easier to share such feelings with people who have a personal understanding.

The development of self-help groups throughout Northern Ireland has provided people with the means to be more involved in their own care. It may be regarded as a "stepping stone" back into community life.

HOW TO BE YOUR OWN BEST FRIEND

- Give yourself a break from doing things for other people.

- Take yourself to lunch or dinner once a week.

- Do any fun, non-routine thing that enters your mind: go roller-skating, read your favourite book or take a walk in the rain without your umbrella.

- Demonstrate your I'm-my-best-friend feelings by treating yourself to a small gift (anything you love books, records, cosmetics) once a month.

- Make your body more lovable. Save up your pennies and spend a week at a spa or health farm.

FOR PEOPLE WITH EATING DISTRESS

Most of us have spent far too much time feeling badly about who we are and what we have done. We may have been harshly criticised by others or we may simply have lost perspective and become overly hard on ourselves. Today we have an opportunity to stop that kind of self-destructive thinking. Isn't it about time we allowed ourselves to feel good about ourselves?

It takes time for old habits and doubts to fade and wounds to heal. Self-confidence comes slowly but grows with practice. We can begin by acknowledging that we do have positive qualities. Those of us who have negative, self-critical thoughts running through our heads all day long can make an extra effort to counteract them with positive thoughts. For every defect we identify we can also try to name an asset. Some of us find it helpful to list five or ten things about our day that we have a right to feel good about before we go to sleep.

With practice we can learn to treat ourselves with gentleness and compassion. We all have many admirable qualities and we owe it to ourselves to let them shine.

Reminder for today: *I will make an effort to remember that I am a terrific human being!!*

AFFIRMATIONS

I am strong and confident

I am a healthy person and I feel good

I am kind and I have plenty to offer everyone

I am now learning to handle my life well

Every step I take is positive and good for me

I will share my happiness with everyone

Every day my life is getting better

My life is very important, because I can help others

Everything I meet in life, whether good or bad, is for my own learning

My life is now more peaceful

I am in control of everything I do

I am strong in mind and body

Every breath I take is full of healing energy

I feel full of healing energy

I feel strong, confident and happy

Use these affirmations first thing in the morning or last thing at night. These positive thought forms, if used with meaning, will rest in the subconscious mind. The positive waves released by affirmations and good thoughts will renew the cell tissues and nerves. What we think is what we are. Thoughts of cheerfulness, joy and courage heal and soothe.

FOOD AND EMOTIONS

When you crave certain foods, be aware of what is happening and know that if you can ride it out, it will surely eventually pass. Make a phone call, go for a walk, have a bath or make a hot drink. Play some nice music that relaxes you.

The problem comes when emotionally-driven food habits take over from healthy eating and result in uncontrolled weight gain.

WHAT IS RECOVERY?

Recovery is learning how to deal with life's problems in constructive ways without turning to food or starvation. Recovery involves learning how to get more out of life while learning how to balance life with other things like friendships, work, hobbies and interests.

Anything that offers hope has the potential to heal. Hope is more powerful than any other therapeutic technique. Recovery is about making better choices in life. It is important to learn not to be afraid of recovery. Instead, focus on learning how to enjoy the journey to find the real self. Recovery involves letting go of the desire to be rescued and taking responsibility to find out who we are.

Recovery is:

- Gaining freedom from food obsession
- Gaining freedom from body obsession
- Learning to know yourself
- Learning to be aware of yourself
- Learning to accept yourself
- Learning to believe in yourself
- Emphasizing honesty
- Living in the present
- Taking care of your physical health
- Changing and being open to forming new relationships
- Giving to others and learning to receive
- Having clarity of thought
- Developing spiritually
- Gaining the ability to have real fun in life
- **Loving yourself the way you are**

EATING DISTRESS IN THE WORKPLACE

Our image and how we are seen by our colleagues and friends seem to dominate daily life. Running parallel is a national preoccupation with food and diet. As a consequence eating distress, such as anorexia and bulimia nervosa, are in the public eye to an extent that would have been unthinkable twenty **You can overcome it** years ago. This has created myths and misunderstandings, a false perception of what someone with an eating distress will look like, and how they will behave at work or at home.

In reality most people with an eating disorder would be difficult to identify. You would never know that there was a problem and would not suspect from their work performance that they had an eating disorder. However, for a small but significant proportion of people with eating distress, food and eating can become a dangerous obsession.

Studies have shown that the earlier an eating disorder is recognised and both treatment and help sought, the better the chances of recovery. You can get better. Recovery is possible even after many years of illness.

It is here that you, as an employer, can play a key role. Your action may be crucial to the future health and well being of the staff member and staff team.

A CARER'S STORY

"One of the people closest to me was now recovering from an Eating Disorder. During those eating disorder years, I had become so enmeshed with her and her self-destructive behaviour that I lost sight of the idea that I could be happy even if she was depressed; that I could live a serene life even if she went back to her eating disorder. The turning point in life came when someone said to me: "You'll have to learn to make it whether your daughter does or not".

From that day on I tried to keep in mind that I had my own life and my own destiny. Once I began to separate my welfare from that of my daughter, I found it easier to detach from the decisions she made about how and where, and when to conduct her life. Because my fate - my very life - was no longer tied directly to her, I was able to accept her for who she was and to listen to her ideas and concerns without trying to exercise control. She was aware I was always there for her, and she only had to ask for my support if she wished to do so.

Thanks to my self-help /support group, I've learned to concentrate my energy where I do have some control - over my own life.

As I continue to practise putting the focus on myself, it is a relief to see that I can let go of others' problems instead of trying to solve them".

HELP FOR PARENTS AND FRIENDS

Maybe you know someone who has anorexia or bulimia nervosa and you are worried. The person may perhaps be your child. Here are some suggestions as to how you might understand and respond helpfully to the situation.

Anorexia and bulimia are outward signs that something is wrong inside. The problem really relates to a crisis about self-identity. Eating disorders provide a way of trying to reach a position of independence when this feels very difficult. Taking control of the body and food intake can seem perhaps the only way of achieving this. As parents or people close to a person with an eating disorder, you can be very helpful in this struggle. But it will not be easy for you! Parents can often feel that home has become a battleground with food as a very powerful weapon. It may seem as though conflicting messages come from the person with the eating disorder to the parents. It sometimes sounds like:

Leave me alone, let me live my own life, I hate you.
Don't ever leave me, I can't cope on my own, I love you.

This kind of ambivalence, these contradictory feelings are hard to live with. It is, however, important to allow these conflicting and painful emotions to be expressed. Periods of depression, anger, hopelessness and despair are all part of the experience of growing up. It is not easy for anyone concerned.

Parents, too, have feelings and may give out conflicting messages. It may sound like:

- *It must be my fault.*
- *I'll do anything to make you better.*
- *I love you so much.*
- *I can't bear to see you unhappy.*
- *I worry about you all the time.*
- *You are ruining my life.*
- *I want to shake you.*
- *At times I hate you.*

Parents often end up feeling guilty and totally responsible for everything which has happened. This is not a good point from which to begin to tackle the problems presented by anorexia or bulimia nervosa.

Parents usually do what they think is best at the time, and everyone can be wise in retrospect. Accept what has happened in the past, and concentrate on what can be done now and in the future.

HOW CAN YOU HELP?

One of the barriers which people with eating disorders have to overcome in order to get help with the problem is their own resistance to acknowledging that the problem is really very complex and there is no short cut to recovery.

- You cannot make the person overcome this barrier, but at least you need not collude with it and look for miracle cures.
- Accept that at present this is the only way the person feels that life is in control, the only way of coping.
- Be prepared to listen and to give time.
- Accept that the person will probably react badly to whatever approach you make - but don't let this put you off doing what you feel is right.
- The person needs affirmation in every way and unconditional acceptance, not just for achievement.
- Don't leave lots of tempting goodies around, or give extra or reduced helpings without being asked. Remember that the aim is to help the body eat what it really needs.
- Try to avoid confrontations about food.
- Seek professional help and persist if it is not forthcoming immediately.
- Read about the problem to increase your understanding.
- The idea of recovery can be frightening, so it is difficult for the person to hear things like "you look better", "good, you've put on weight". Her response to this sort of comment is likely to be "I've put on weight - help - if I don't lose it again quickly I'll get fat".
- Accept that character changes are part of the illness. The person may become deceitful or start shoplifting. She needs to be helped rather than judged.

Progress may mean difficulties between parents and the person with the eating disorder because it will involve a more assertive attitude and a degree of separation. This will be a struggle for all of you. It may be a temporary period of difficulty whilst changes are being made. You may feel that you as well as the sufferer need some counselling, or other help with your own feelings.

Don't be afraid to ask. Progress requires change.

For the men in the family

The person with the eating disorder and the rest of the family need your help. Don't opt out by thinking this is "women's work". Try to share your feelings, ideas, work, and leisure with the rest of the family. Accept them as equals and respect their view so that they feel happy sharing their experiences with you too.

Useful literature

ANOREXIA NERVOSA, by R. L. Palmer, published by Penguin Books

FAMILIES AND HOW TO SURVIVE THEM, by John Cleese and Robin Skinner, published by Methuen Paperbacks

ANOREXIA AND BULIMIA - HOW TO HELP, by Marilyn Duker & Roger Slade, published by Open University Press.

Acknowledgement: Eating Disorders Association, First Floor, Wensum House, 103 Prince of Wales Road, Norwich NR1 1DW

HOW I MIGHT CONTRIBUTE TO EATING DISTRESS

- Admire weight loss diets.

- Encourage perfectionism in self and others.

- Admire rigidly controlled eating.

- Encourage someone else to pursue a diet that deprives them of fattening foods .

- Tease someone about their eating habits.

- Criticise your own eating habits or choices.

- Make negative comments about your own or somebody else's "fatness".

- Support the assumption that no one should be "fat".

- Say or assume someone is doing well because of weight loss.

- Say something that presumes that bigger people should lose weight.

- Say something that presumes that bigger people eat too much.

- Refer to good and bad foods.

- Talking about "being good" and "being bad" in reference to eating behaviour.

- Admire thinness.

- Make weight important.

- Admire excessive exercise.

Poems

IT

It keeps me safe
It's my friend
It stops me feeling
It answers questions
It stops me growing
It means I don't have to
Face truths
I'd rather not know

Please don't challenge "IT"
Because then you're challenging me.

A Sufferer

Fuel
Undeniably
Essential for
Life

I've learned that everyone has qualities and should not be judged by their size.

Fat
Ordinary or like a
Rake   *Joan*

Risk

To laugh is to risk appearing a fool
To weep is to risk appearing sentimental
To reach out to another is to risk involvement
To expose feelings is to risk exposing your true self
To place your ideas, your dreams, before the crowd is to risk their loss
To love is to risk not being loved in return
To live is to risk dying
To hope is to risk despair
To try is to risk failure

But risks must be taken because the greatest hazard in life is to risk nothing. Those who risk nothing do nothing, have nothing, and are nothing. They may avoid suffering and sorrow, but they simply cannot learn, feel, change, grow, love, live. Chained by their certitude, they are slaves, they have forfeited freedom. Only a person who risks is free.

Sufferer

I'm staring, I'm falling,
I'm searching, I'm crying.
I'm hungry, I'm lying.

I'm staring, I'm falling,
I'm controlling, I'm trying
I give in then I'm purging
I'm guilty, I'm lying.

I'm staring, I'm falling,
I'm falling, I'm falling.
I'm lost, I'm scared,
I'm alone . . . SOS I'm calling.

I'm accepting, I'm talking.
I'm listening, I'm trying.
I slip and I'm falling,
I'm frustrated.
They're sighing.

They listen, they support,
They nudge and they aid.
I can't let them down,
As through my dark waters
they wade.

I'm staring, I've fallen.
I'm thinking. I'm praying.
Do I want to get out of this at
all?
Eventually I decide that in
hell I'm NOT staying.

I'm staring but I don't fall.
Fall a little . . . then I stall.
I'm strong now and I'm
ready,
Hold someone's hand and at
last I'm steady.

Time it passes.
The thoughts begin to fade.
Memories haunt and linger
But now I can be someone's
aid.

THINK POSITIVE

If you think you are beaten, you are.
If you think you dare not, you don't.
Success begins with your own will,
It's all in your state of mind.
Life's battles are not always won by
Those who are stronger or faster.
Sooner or later the person who wins
Is the person who thinks "I can!"

GOOD NEWS

When did you last read in the newspaper headlines like "Person cured of terminal disease", "Reunited families helping one another", "People being visited in hospital", "Person in difficulties helped"?

Good news is not news in our media. It is like in nature: something so beautiful as a daffodil is common and we do not stop and wonder. We sometimes worship negativity too much. It excites us and we are programmed for it by society. One of the reasons why eating disorders are on the increase is because we are surrounded by more negativity than we can handle. We absorb it on an unconscious level and it causes us a lot of anxiety. Our minds get re-trained to react more to the negative and we are unable to appreciate the opposite.

Today will be your "looking for good news day". When you read your paper or when you talk to people, concentrate on the good news. Ask more about it, bring it to other people's attention that there are good things happening in the world and that we all need to be made aware of this news as much as the atrocities that surround us on a daily basis.

HOW CAN I LOOK AFTER MY MENTAL HEALTH?

Regular bedtimes

Getting sleep and rest are vital.

Good diet - "You are what you eat".

If you eat a healthy diet you will be healthy.

Enough Exercise

Create a plan, start with two 20-30 minutes of exercise each week: walk, swim, check what's on in your local leisure centre.

Less caffeine / alcohol & cigarettes.

You may need help to tackle these habits and disorders.

Learn to relax

Take time to relax, e.g. soak in a bath, listen to music, and take up a hobby or pastime, yoga.

What is good mental health?

Good mental health isn't just the absence of mental health problems.

Individuals with good mental health:

- Develop emotionally, creatively, intellectually and spiritually.

- Initiate, develop and sustain mutually satisfying personal relationships.

- Face problems, resolve them and learn from them.

- Are confident and assertive.

- Are aware of others and empathise with them.

- Use and enjoy solitude.

- Play and have fun.

- Laugh, both at themselves and at the world.

ARE YOU BEING BULLIED?

If so:

- Don't put up with bullying.

- Do tell a friend.

- Do tell an adult.

- If you are a young person do tell your parents.

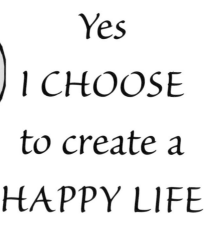

Yes

I CHOOSE

to create a

HAPPY LIFE

....

The PAST is History,

The FUTURE is a mystery.

The PRESENT

MOMENT ...

Is a GIFT.

never give up

That's why it's called ...

'THE PRESENT'

And the gift is YOURS for the taking!

Quotes from sufferers:

"Recovery from an eating disorder is not easy by any means. There are times when my mood is low and I reach for the familarity of bulimia. My willpower is strong though and any "relapse" is very brief. It is my positive mind that encourages me to persist in my goal. I know that it will take a long time before gradually my obsession with food and weight slips into the background. I am learning to value myself for the individual that I am, and not a number on the scales."

"Suffering and fighting an eating disorder may be one of the most difficult experiences one is faced with throughout one's life."

"For me at 21 years of age, I will state that it is the most challenging experience that I have been faced with so far in life. However, from having faith in myself, being determined and reassuring myself each day that I can win this battle and that I will overcome this journey, each day is getting better and easier."

"However hard it may be, **do not give up**."

"You can do this as much as the next person."

Towards Recovery

"My first step towards recovery was acknowledging that I had a problem, and having the courage to visit my GP. My GP didn't judge me but gave me hope and referred me to a specialist clinic. With time I was able to open up to a few friends, who acted with support, love and understanding. With guidance from my therapist, I understood that eating regularly and healthily dispels physiological cravings and prevents weight fluctuations. As I progress through recovery, I feel more and more empowered. I am starting to feel good about myself, something that is much more fulfiling than my previous destructive behaviour."

A Sufferer

The earlier an eating disorder is recognised and both help and treatment sought, the better the chances of recovery. You can get better: **"recovery is possible even after many years of the illness"**.

VICTIM ROLE

"When I am troubled by another person's behaviour, a complicated situation, or a disappointing turn of events, my self-help/support group members remind me that I don't have to take it personally. I am not a victim of everything that happens unless I choose to see myself that way. Though things don't always go my way, I can accept what I cannot change and change what I can!

Perhaps I can take a different view of the situation (problem). If I accept them on face value without taking them personally, I may find that they are not problems at all and the situation not quite as bad as I first thought, only things have not gone as I would have liked. This change of attitude can help free me to evaluate the situation realistically and move forward constructively.

Reminder

Blaming my discomfort on outside events can be a way to avoid facing the real cause - my own attitudes. I can see myself as a victim, or I can accept what is happening in my life and take responsibility for my response. I may be guided to take actions or to sit still".

A Carer

STRESS MANAGEMENT

Stress Busters

PHYSICAL ACTIVITY

Regular exercise helps you feel fit, relaxed and gives you more energy.

Benefits of Physical Activity

- Improves brain function
- Enhances feelings of self-esteem and well-being
- Helps with weight control
- Makes for a healthier lifestyle
- Lowers the risk of disease and diabetes in later life

AIM: to accumulate at least 30 minutes of moderate physical activity every day (brisk walking, gardening, cycling, swimming, dancing, etc).

Tips to include more activity in your life

- Start walking to college
- Use the stairs - not the lift

RELAPSE WARNING SIGNS

✓ INCREASE IN OBSESSIVE THINKING ABOUT FOOD AND WEIGHT

✓ WANTING TO BE IN CONTROL ALL THE TIME

✓ PERFECTIONIST ATTITUDES

✓ WANTING TO ESCAPE FROM STRESSFUL SITUATIONS

✓ FEELING HOPELESS ABOUT WORK, RELATIONSHIPS OR LIFE

✓ BELIEVING YOU WILL BE HAPPY AND SUCCESSFUL IF THIN

✓ FEELING OF BEING "TOO FAT", EVEN THOUGH PEOPLE SAY OTHERWISE

✓ WANTING TO ISOLATE

✓ UNABLE TO USE YOUR SUPPORT SYSTEMS

✓ BEING DISHONEST WITH THOSE HELPING YOU ABOUT YOUR SYMPTOMS

✓ LOOKING IN THE MIRROR OFTEN

✓ DAILY WEIGHING

RELAPSE WARNING SIGNS

✓ AVOIDING CERTAIN FOODS BECAUSE OF THE CALORIE CONTENT

✓ PURCHASING MOSTLY DIET FOODS

✓ SKIPPING MEALS

✓ EXCESSIVE EXERCISING

✓ WEARING ONLY LOOSE-FITTING CLOTHES

✓ THOUGHTS OF SUICIDE

✓ FEELING DISGUSTED WITH ONESELF AFTER EATING

Adapt

Anorexia & Bulimia Nervosa Self-Help/Support Group

Meets:

On the last Thursday of every month @ 7.30pm
(Except July & December)

Venue:

37 High Street, Lurgan, BT66 8AH

Phone:

028 3834 7535

EVERYONE WELCOME

Helpline:

028 3834 8869

NOTES